SLOW COOKER COOKBOOK

1200 Days of Easy & Delicious Slow Cooker Homemade Meals Recipes To Enjoy with Your Family and Friends

Poula Ray

Table of Contents

1. Introduction

The busy schedule of our life doesn't leave much time for cooking. However, each of us wants to eat healthy and delicious meals. Getting this, you need a responsible approach. Why do you need to choose the slow cooker? It perfectly copes both with complicated and simple recipes, while eliminating the need of controlling the cooking process and spending much time in the kitchen.

The device will never be superfluous, as it can cook almost all your favorite meals but in a healthier way. The most popular ingredients to cook in the slow cooker are:

- meat and poultry;
- fish;
- vegetables;
- soups;
- stuffing;
- porridge
- jams
- broths
- desserts

You should bear in mind that the cooking process in the slow cooker has to be started long before eating time. You can do all preparations at one certain time and forget about cooking for the rest of the day. Correctly using the slow cooker in your kitchen and cooking according to the recipes from this cookbook, you are doomed to success!

The slow cooker is a fairly easy-to-use kitchen equipment that doesn't require professional cooking skills. The process of cooking will be easy for all people: busy professionals, teenagers, etc.

How does it work? Everything is very easy. Firstly, you need to put food in a slow cooker bowl. The hull of the slow cooker is made of stainless steel, while inside it is supplemented with a ceramic bowl so that the food doesn't burn. After you put the food inside, cover it with a lid.

The next step will actually be the selection of the desired cooking mode: normal or high. After this, you can forget about cooking for a few hours and spend time for yourself. The slow cooker will automatically turn off after the meal is completely cooked. As usual, the slow cooker models have a timer that will give you an audible signal and notify when the meal is cooked.

The fact that during cooking it is allowed to open the lid at any time to add ingredients to the meal or, if desired, control the process, gives the extra points in favor of the slow cooker. As usual, the slow cooker lid is made of heat-resistant glass; so you can oversee the cooking process easily.

There are two types of slow cookers: with sensor screen and with buttons. Both options don't change the main features of the slow cooker significantly.

Cleaning the slow cooker is a simple process. You will need minimal effort. Since the slow cooker bowl is non-stick and cooking occurs with a small amount or without fat, cleaning will take a minimum of time. The slow cooker bowl and lid can be washed in a dishwashing machine or with sponge and detergent by hands.

To sum up all the pros and cons of the slow cooker, it is safe to say that the kitchen appliance has more positive sides than negative once. The few disadvantages that are possible to determine are short cord and lack of timer on some models of the slow cooker.

However, the advantages of a slow cooker make it an indispensable tool in the kitchen. Let's sum the advantages up:

- You don't spend much time for cooking. You can calmly spend time with your beloved once, work, or take rest while the meal is cooking;
- The principle of the slow cooker work doesn't let the meal overboil, overflow or burn out;
- Perfect for toddlers. Cooking the vitamin fruit puree without sugar is possible at home. The slow cooker will care about every member of your family;
- due to the optimum temperature and long cooking time, the slow cooker will save all the useful vitamins and minerals. It also helps preserve the taste and aroma of the cooked meal;
- suitable for cooking broths, condensed milk, jams, confitures, and preserves.

According to the pros of the slow cooker that were listed above, it is possible to conclude that it is a unique kitchen appliance with an unusual way of cooking. The slow cooker is a modern substitutor of the old stove where food was cooked on the firewood. Looks amazing, doesn't it? You can stew the ingredients in the slow cooker for many hours and at the same time, your meal will be succulent and save the soft texture. The kitchen appliance is a wonderful discovery for people who follow a healthy lifestyle, a strict diet or have some health problems. It can be good also for cooking food for toddlers and making desserts. As you can see the kitchen appliance is perfect for everyone!

A slow cooker will be an indispensable assistant in your kitchen and this cookbook will help you to impress your beloved with new gorgeous meals day by day!

Chapter 1:   The Basics of Slow Cooking

Slow cookers prepare meals at a low temperature for 4 to 8 hours. The nutrients in the meal remain in the food because of the lower temperature. Any nutrients lost in the liquid due to heat are simply reabsorbed into the food being in a sealed unit, whether using an electric slow cooker or a casserole dish in the oven. Cooking for longer periods of time enhances flavour and eliminates the need for additional seasoning or sauces. Spices and herbs, on the other hand, provide richness by imparting their goodness and aroma to the food.

Benefits of Slow Cooking

While the slow cooker isn't ideal for every cooking method, it does provide a number of major benefits by offering an effortless slow cooking experience. If you are planning to buy a slow cooker, keep reading to learn about some of the advantages of slow cooking.

- The lower cooking temperatures reduce the risk of burning the food items that tend to stick to the bottom of a pan or burn in an oven.

- Tough cheap meats, such as chuck steaks, roast, and less-lean stewing cattle, are tenderized by the long slow cooking.

- For many venison meals, the slow cooker is an ideal choice. The slow cooker keeps your oven and stovetop free for other cooking, and it's an excellent choice for large parties or holiday meals.

- Scrubbing many pots and pans is unnecessary. Most of the time, you'll only have to clean the slow cooker and a few prep items.

- Slow cookers consume less energy than conventional electric ovens.

- Unlike a huge oven, the slow cooker does not heat up the kitchen, which is a big bonus on a hot summer day.

- A slow cooker is easy to transport. It can be taken from the kitchen to the office or to a party. Simply plug it in and eat.

- A slow cooker can be easily left unattended all day. Before going to work, you can put the ingredients for a recipe in it and come home to supper. Whether you work from home or not, a slow cooker meal is a wonderful alternative for a hectic day.

Chapter 2:   Breakfast Recipes

Recipe 1:   Apples and Pears Bowls

Serving Size: 2

Cooking Time: 6 hours

Ingredients:

- 2 apples, cored, peeled and cut into medium chunks
- ½ teaspoon lemon juice
- 2 pears, cored, peeled and cut into medium chunks
- 2 teaspoons sugar
- ¼ teaspoon cinnamon powder
- ½ teaspoon vanilla extract
- ¼ teaspoon ginger, ground
- ¼ teaspoon cloves, ground
- ¼ teaspoon cardamom, ground

Directions:

1. In your slow cooker, mix apples with pears, lemon juice, sugar, cinnamon, vanilla extract, ginger, cloves and cardamom, stir, cover and cook on Low for 6 hours.
2. Divide into bowls and serve for breakfast.
3. Enjoy!

Nutritional Value: Calories 201; Fat 3g; Carbohydrates 19g; Protein 4g

Recipe 2:   Aromatic Wild Rice Pilaf

Serving Size: 12

Cooking Time: 7 hours

Ingredients:

- ½ cup wild rice
- ½ cup barley
- 2/3 cup wheat berries
- 27 ounces vegetable stock
- 2 cups baby lima beans
- 1 red bell pepper, chopped
- 1 yellow onion, chopped
- 1 tablespoon olive oil
- 1 teaspoon sage, dried and crushed
- 4 garlic cloves, minced

Directions:

1. In your Slow cooker, mix rice with barley, wheat berries, lima beans, bell pepper, onion, oil, sage, and garlic, stir, cover, and cook on Low for 7 hours.
2. Stir one more time, divide between plates and serve as a side dish.

Nutritional Value: Calories 115; Fat 1.8g; Carbohydrates 21g; Protein 4.7g

Recipe 3:   Bacon and Egg Casserole

Serving Size: 8

Cooking Time: 5 hours

Ingredients:

- 20 ounces hash browns
- Cooking spray
- 8 ounces cheddar cheese, shredded
- 8 bacon slices, cooked and chopped
- 6 green onions, chopped
- ½ cup milk
- 12 eggs
- Salt and black pepper to the taste
- Salsa for serving

Directions:

1. Grease your Slow cooker with cooking spray, spread hash browns, cheese, bacon and green onions and toss.
2. In a bowl, mix the eggs with salt, pepper and milk and whisk really well.
3. Pour this over hash browns, cover and cook on Low for 5 hours.
4. Divide between plates and serve with salsa on top.

Nutritional Value: Calories 300; Fat 5g; Carbohydrates 9g; Protein 5g

Recipe 4:   Breakfast Butterscotch Pudding

Serving Size: 6

Cooking Time: 1 hour 40 minutes

Ingredients:

- 4 ounces butter, melted
- 2 ounces brown sugar
- 7 ounces flour
- ¼ pint milk
- 1 teaspoon vanilla extract
- Zest of ½ lemon, grated
- 2 tablespoons maple syrup
- Cooking spray
- 1 egg

Directions:

1. In a bowl, mix butter with sugar, milk, vanilla, lemon zest, maple syrup and eggs and whisk well.
2. Add flour and whisk really well again.
3. Grease your Slow cooker with cooking spray, add pudding mix, spread, cover and cook on High for 1 hour and 30 minutes.
4. Divide between plates and serve for breakfast.

Nutritional Value: Calories 271; Fat 5g; Carbohydrates 17g; Protein 4g

Recipe 5: Breakfast Pork Meatloaf

Serving Size: 2

Cooking Time: 3 hours

Ingredients:

- ½ yellow onion, chopped
- 1 pound pork, minced
- ½ teaspoon red pepper flakes
- ½ teaspoon olive oil
- 1 garlic clove, minced
- 2 tablespoons white flour
- ½ teaspoon oregano, chopped
- ½ tablespoon sage, minced
- A pinch of salt and black pepper
- ½ tablespoon sweet paprika
- ½ teaspoon marjoram, dried
- 1 egg

Directions:

1. In a bowl, mix pork with salt, pepper, onion, garlic, pepper flakes, flour, oregano, sage, paprika, marjoram and egg, stir well and shape your meatloaf.
2. Grease a loaf pan that fits your slow cooker with the oil, add meatloaf mix, spread well, transfer the pan to your slow cooker, cover and cook on Low for 3 hours.
3. Leave aside to actually cool down, slice and serve for breakfast.
4. Enjoy!

Nutritional Value: Calories 200; Fat 6g; Carbohydrates 17g; Protein 10g

Recipe 6:   Breakfast Yams

Serving Size: 2

Cooking Time: 2 hours

Ingredients:

- 2 yams, peeled and cut into chunks
- 2/3 cup walnuts, chopped
- 2 cups basil, chopped
- 1 garlic clove, minced
- ½ cup olive oil
- Juice of ½ lemon
- A pinch of salt and black pepper

Directions:

1. In your blender, combine the walnuts with basil, garlic, oil, lemon juice, salt and pepper and pulse well.
2. Put the yams in your slow cooker, add the walnuts pesto, toss, cover, cook on Low for 2 hours, divide into bowls and serve for breakfast.
3. Enjoy!

Nutritional Value: Calories 221; Fat 4g; Carbohydrates 17g; Protein 8g

Recipe 7:   Broccoli Egg Casserole

Serving Size: 5

Cooking Time: 3 hours

Ingredients:

- 4 eggs, beaten
- ½ cup full-fat milk
- 3 tablespoons grass-fed butter, melted
- 1 ½ cup broccoli florets, chopped
- Salt and pepper to taste

Directions:

1. Beat the prepared eggs and milk in a mixing bowl.
2. Grease the bottom of the CrockPot with melted butter.
3. Add in the broccoli florets in the CrockPot and pour the egg mixture.
4. Season with salt and pepper to taste.
5. Close the lid and cook on high for 2 hours or on low for 3 hours.

Nutritional Value: Calories 217; Fat 16.5g; Carbohydrates 4.6g; Protein 11.6g

Recipe 8:   Butternut Squash Bowls

Serving Size: 3

Cooking Time: 6 hours

Ingredients:

- 1 banana, peeled and chopped
- 1 teaspoon cinnamon powder
- 1 cup coconut, shredded
- ½ cup butternut squash puree
- ½ cup coconut milk

Directions:

1. In your slow cooker, combine the banana with the cinnamon, coconut, squash puree and coconut milk, toss, cover and cook on Low for 6 hours.
2. Divide into bowls and serve for breakfast.
3. Enjoy!

Nutritional Value: Calories 210; Fat 8g; Carbohydrates 15g; Protein 6g

Recipe 9:   Cajun Beef and Sausage Stuffed Peppers

Serving Size: 6

Cooking Time: 3 hours

Ingredients:

- 12 ounces (70% lean) ground beef
- 12 ounces andouille sausage, finely diced
- 11/2 cups shredded Cheddar cheese, divided
- 1/2 cup almond meal
- 2 celery stalks, finely diced
- 1 onion, finely diced
- 4 garlic cloves, minced
- 1 teaspoon dried oregano
- 1 teaspoon paprika
- 1 teaspoon kosher salt
- 1/2 teaspoon freshly ground black pepper
- 1/4 teaspoon cayenne pepper
- 1 bell peppers (any color), halved through the stem, seeded and ribbed
- 1/4 cup beef broth

Directions:

1. In a large bowl, mix the onion, beef, sausage, black pepper, almond meal, oregano, celery, paprika, garlic, salt, 1 cup of Cheddar cheese, and cayenne pepper. Spoon the meat mixture into the pepper halves, dividing equally. Place the stuffed peppers in the slow cooker.
2. Pour the beef broth around the peppers.
3. Sprinkle with the remaining 1/2 cup of Cheddar cheese. Cover and cook for 7 hours on low. Serve hot.

Nutritional Value: Calories 217; Fat 16.3g; Carbohydrates 3.4g; Protein 14.7g

Recipe 10: Chai Quinoa

Serving Size: 6

Cooking Time: 6 hours

Ingredients:

- 1 cup quinoa
- 1 egg white
- 2 cups of coconut milk
- ¼ teaspoon vanilla extract
- 1 tablespoon honey
- ¼ teaspoon cardamom, ground
- ¼ teaspoon ginger, grated
- ¼ teaspoon ground cinnamon
- ¼ teaspoon vanilla extract
- ¼ teaspoon nutmeg, ground
- 1 tablespoon coconut flakes

Directions:

1. In your Slow cooker, mix quinoa with egg white, milk, vanilla, honey, cardamom, ginger, cinnamon, vanilla, and nutmeg, stir a bit, cover and cook on Low for 6 hours.
2. Stir, divide into bowls, and serve for breakfast with coconut flakes on top.

Nutritional Value: Calories 307; Fat 21.1g; Carbohydrates 25.9g; Protein 6.5g

Recipe 11: Cheesy Potato-Broccoli Soup

Serving Size: 6

Cooking Time: 2 hours

Ingredients:

- 2 pounds red or Yukon potatoes, chopped
- 1(10-ounce) bag frozen broccoli
- 2cups unsweetened nondairy milk
- 1small yellow onion, chopped
- 11/2 teaspoons minced garlic (3 cloves)
- 3vegetable bouillon cubes
- 4cups water
- 1cup meltable vegan Cheddar-cheese shreds
- Pinch salt
- Freshly ground black pepper to taste

Directions:

1. Combine the potatoes, broccoli, nondairy milk, onion, garlic, bouillon cubes, and water in a slow cooker; mix well.
2. Cover and cook on low for 5 to 7 hours or on high for 3 to 4 hours.
3. Forty-five minutes before serving, use an immersion blender (or a regular blender, working in batches) to blend the soup until it's nice and creamy.
4. Stir in the vegan cheese, cover, and cook for another 45 minutes.
5. Season with salt and pepper.

Nutritional Value: Calories 283; Fat 11.9g; Carbohydrates 28.8g; Protein 25.4g

Recipe 12: Cherry Oats

Serving Size: 2

Cooking Time: 8 hours

Ingredients:

- 1 cup milk
- 1 cup water
- ½ cup steel cut oats
- 1 tablespoon cocoa powder
- ¼ cup cherries, pitted
- 2 tablespoons maple syrup
- ¼ teaspoon almond extract

Directions:

1. In your slow cooker, combine milk with water, oats, cocoa powder, cherries, maples syrup and almond extract, stir, cover and cook on Low for 8 hours.
2. Divide into 2 bowls and serve for breakfast.
3. Enjoy!

Nutritional Value: Calories 150; Fat 1g; Carbohydrates 6g; Protein 5g

Recipe 13: Cream Cheese Banana Breakfast

Serving Size: 2

Cooking Time: 4 hours

Ingredients:

- ½ French baguette, sliced
- 2 bananas, sliced
- 2 ounces cream cheese
- 1 tablespoon brown sugar
- ¼ cup walnuts, chopped
- 1 egg, whisked
- 3 tablespoons skim milk
- 2 tablespoons honey
- ½ teaspoon cinnamon powder
- A pinch of nutmeg, ground
- ¼ teaspoon vanilla extract
- 1 tablespoon butter
- Cooking spray

Directions:

1. Spread cream cheese on all bread slices and grease your slow cooker with Cooking spray.
2. Arrange bread slices in your slow cooker, layer banana slices, brown sugar and walnuts.
3. In a bowl, mix eggs with skim milk, honey, cinnamon, nutmeg and vanilla extract, whisk and add over bread slices.
4. Add butter, cover, cook on Low for 4 hours, divide between plates and serve for breakfast.
5. Enjoy!

Nutritional Value: Calories 251; Fat 5g; Carbohydrates 12g; Protein 4g

Recipe 14: Feta Mushroom Casserole

Serving Size: 2

Cooking Time: 4 hours

Ingredients:

- ½ teaspoon lemon zest, grated
- 3 ounces feta cheese, crumbled
- ½ tablespoon lemon juice
- 2 eggs, whisked
- ½ tablespoon apple cider vinegar
- ½ tablespoon olive oil
- 1 garlic cloves, minced
- 4 ounces spinach, torn
- 2 tablespoons yellow onion, chopped
- ¼ teaspoon basil, dried
- 3 ounces mushrooms, sliced
- Salt and black pepper to the taste
- A pinch of red pepper flakes
- Cooking spray

Directions:

1. In a bowl, mix eggs with salt, olive oil, lemon juice, pepper vinegar, garlic, pepper flakes onion, mushrooms, basil, lemon zest, and and spinach, whisk well.
2. Grease your slow cooker with cooking spray, add eggs mix, sprinkle cheese all over, cover and cook on Low for 4 hours.
3. Divide between plates and serve for breakfast.
4. Enjoy!

Nutritional Value: Calories 216; Fat 6g; Carbohydrates 12g; Protein 4g

Recipe 15: French Breakfast Pudding

Serving Size: 4

Cooking Time: 1 hour 30 minutes

Ingredients:

- 3 egg yolks
- 6 ounces double cream
- 1 teaspoon vanilla extract
- 2 tablespoons caster sugar

Directions:

1. In a large-sized bowl, mix the egg yolks with sugar and whisk well.
2. Add cream and vanilla extract, whisk well, pour into your 4 ramekins, place them in your Slow Cooker, add some water to the Slow Cooker, cover and cook on High for 1 hour and 30 minutes.
3. Leave aside to cool down and serve.

Nutritional Value: Calories 261; Fat 5g; Carbohydrates 15g; Protein 2g

Recipe 16: Honey and Soy Sauce Chicken Wings

Serving Size: 6

Cooking Time: 7 hours

Ingredients:

- 1 teaspoon chili powder
- 20 chicken wings
- 1 c. soy sauce
- 1 c. honey
- 2 c. brown sugar
- 1 teaspoon lemon juice
- 1 teaspoon Worcestershire sauce
- 1 teaspoon ground ginger
- 1 teaspoon salt
- 1 teaspoon pepper

Directions:

1. In your mixing bowl, mix everything except the chicken wings.
2. Put half of the mixture into the slow cooker.
3. Add the chicken wings in the slow cooker and cover with the rest of the sauce.
4. Cook on low for 6 - 7 hours.

Nutritional Value: Calories 207; Fat 1.5g; Carbohydrates 25.5g; Protein 4g

Recipe 17: Mac and Cheese with Bacon

Serving Size: 18

Cooking Time: 25 minutes

Ingredients:

- 2 lightly beaten eggs, large
- 4 cups of milk, whole
- 1 x 12-oz. can of milk, evaporated
- 1/4 cup of melted butter, unsalted
- 1 tablespoon of flour, all-purpose
- 1 teaspoon of salt, kosher
- 1 x 16-oz. pkg. of pasta shells, small
- 1 cup of provolone cheese shreds
- 1 cup of Monterey jack cheese shreds
- 1 cup of white cheddar cheese shreds
- 8 cooked, crumbled strips of bacon

Directions:

1. In a large-sized bowl, whisk the first six ingredients together till blended well. Stir in cheeses and pasta. Transfer to your slow cooker.
2. Cover slow cooker. Cook on low for 3 – 3 & 1/2 hours or till pasta becomes tender. Turn the slow cooker off. Remove the insert and leave it uncovered. Allow it to stand for 15-18 minutes. Top with bacon and serve.

Nutritional Value: Calories 228; Fat 10g; Carbohydrates 18g; Protein 24g

Recipe 18: Milky Broccoli Omelet

Serving Size: 2

Cooking Time: 2 hours

Ingredients:

- Cooking spray
- 3 eggs, whisked
- ¼ cup milk
- A pinch of salt and black pepper
- A pinch of garlic powder
- A pinch of chili powder
- ½ cup broccoli florets
- ½ red bell pepper, chopped
- ½ yellow onion, chopped
- 1 small garlic clove, minced
- 1 tomato, chopped
- 1 tablespoon parsley, chopped

Directions:

1. In a bowl, mix eggs with milk, salt, pepper, chili powder, garlic powder, broccoli, bell pepper, onion and garlic and whisk really well.
2. Grease your slow cooker with cooking spray, pour eggs mix, spread, cover and cook on High for 2 hours.
3. Slice into halves, divide omelet between plates, sprinkle tomato and parsley on top and serve for breakfast.
4. Enjoy!

Nutritional Value: Calories 162; Fat 5g; Carbohydrates 15g; Protein 4g

Recipe 19: Oats Granola

Serving Size: 8

Cooking Time: 2 hours

Ingredients:

- 5 cups old-fashioned rolled oats
- 1/3 cup coconut oil
- 2/3 cup honey
- ½ cup almonds, chopped
- ½ cup peanut butter
- 1 tablespoon vanilla
- 2 teaspoons cinnamon powder
- 1 cup craisins
- Cooking spray

Directions:

1. Grease your Slow cooker with cooking spray, add oats, oil, honey, almonds, peanut butter, vanilla, craisins and cinnamon, toss just a bit, cover and cook on High for 2 hours, stirring every 30 minutes.
2. Divide into bowls and serve for breakfast.

Nutritional Value: Calories 200; Fat 3g; Carbohydrates 9g; Protein 4g

Recipe 20: Onion Frittata

Serving Size: 4

Cooking Time: 2 hours

Ingredients:

- A pinch of white pepper
- 1 tablespoon olive oil
- ½ cup yellow onion, chopped
- 1 cup low-fat cheese, shredded
- 1 cup baby spinach leaves
- 1 tomato, chopped
- 3 egg whites
- 3 eggs
- 2 tablespoon low-fat milk
- A pinch of black pepper

Directions:

1. In a bowl, mix the eggs with the egg whites, milk, white and black pepper, spinach and tomato and stir.
2. Grease the slow cooker with the oil, pour eggs mix, spread the cheese on top, cover and cook on Low for 2 hours.
3. Slice the frittata, divide between plates and serve.

Nutritional Value: Calories 217; Fat 16.3g; Carbohydrates 3.4g; Protein 14.7g

Recipe 21: Pumpkin Oatmeal

Serving Size: 4

Cooking Time: 9 hours

Ingredients:

- Cooking spray
- 1 cup steel-cut oats
- ½ cup organic almond milk
- 4 cups of water
- 2 tablespoons honey
- ½ cup pumpkin puree
- ½ teaspoon cinnamon powder
- A pinch of cloves, ground
- A pinch of ginger, grated
- A pinch of allspice, ground
- A pinch of nutmeg, ground

Directions:

1. Grease your Slow cooker with cooking spray, add oats, milk, water, honey, pumpkin puree, cinnamon, cloves, ginger, allspice, and nutmeg, cover, and cook on Low for 9 hours.
2. Stir your oatmeal, divide into bowls and serve for breakfast.

Nutritional Value: Calories 99; Fat 1.6g; Carbohydrates 20.1g; Protein 2.1g

Recipe 22: Quinoa Spinach Casserole

Serving Size: 2

Cooking Time: 4 hours

Ingredients:

- ¼ cup quinoa
- 1 cup milk
- 2 eggs
- A pinch of salt and black pepper
- ¼ cup spinach, chopped
- ¼ cup cherry tomatoes, halved
- 2 tablespoons cheddar cheese, shredded
- 2 tablespoons parmesan, shredded
- Cooking spray

Directions:

1. In a bowl, mix eggs with quinoa, milk, salt, pepper, tomatoes, spinach and cheddar cheese and whisk well.
2. Grease your slow cooker with cooking spray, add eggs and quinoa mix, spread parmesan all over, cover and cook on High for 4 hours.
3. Divide between plates and serve.
4. Enjoy!

Nutritional Value: Calories 251; Fat 5g; Carbohydrates 19g; Protein 11g

Recipe 23: Sausage and Sweet Pepper Hash

Serving Size: 10

Cooking Time: 3 hours

Ingredients:

- ¾ (12 oz.) package cooked smoked chicken sausage, quartered lengthwise and cut into ½-inch pieces
- 1 teaspoon olive oil
- 1½ cups sliced sweet onion
- Nonstick cooking spray
- 1½ lbs. new potatoes, cut into ½-inch pieces
- 2 teaspoon Snipped fresh thyme or ½ teaspoon Dried thyme, crushed
- ½ teaspoon black Pepper
- ¼ cup reduced-sodium chicken broth
- 2 cups chopped green, red, and sweet yellow peppers
- ½ cup shredded Swiss cheese (2 oz.) (optional)
- 2 teaspoon snipped fresh tarragon or parsley

Directions:

1. On medium heat, cook sausage in a big non-stick pan for 5 mins until brown; take the sausage out of the pan; on medium-low heat, heat oil in the same pan. Cook and stir onion for 5 mins until the onion is tender and begins to turn brown.
2. Grease using cooking spray or place a disposable liner at the base of a 3 1/2 or 4qt slow cooker. Mix black pepper, sausage, thyme, onion, and potatoes in the prepared slow cooker; pour in broth.
3. Set on low heat and cook, covered, for 5-6hrs or cook for 2 1/2-3 hours on high heat. Mix in sweet peppers; add cheese if desired.
4. If set on low heat, adjust the cooker to high heat mode. Cook for another 15 mins while covered. Serve using a slotted spoon; add tarragon on top.

Nutritional Value: Calories 260; Fat 11g; Carbohydrates 5g; Protein 20g

Recipe 24: Seafood Eggs

Serving Size: 4

Cooking Time: 2 hours 30 minutes

Ingredients:

- 4 eggs, beaten
- 2 tablespoons cream cheese
- 1 teaspoon Italian seasonings
- 6 oz shrimps, peeled
- 1 teaspoon olive oil

Directions:

1. Mix cream cheese with eggs.
2. Add Italian seasonings and shrimps.
3. Then brush the ramekins with olive oil and pour the egg mixture inside.
4. Transfer the ramekins in the Slow Cooker.
5. Cook the eggs on High for 2.5 hours.

Nutritional Value: Calories 144; Fat 8.4g; Carbohydrates 1.3g; Protein 15.6g

Recipe 25: Spiced Oatmeal

Serving Size: 10

Cooking Time: 9 hours

Ingredients:

- 1 cup steel cut oats
- 2 tablespoons stevia
- ½ teaspoon cinnamon powder
- A pinch of cloves, ground
- ½ cup pumpkin puree
- 4 cups water
- Olive oil cooking spray
- ½ cup fat-free milk
- A pinch of nutmeg, ground
- A pinch of allspice, ground
- A pinch of ginger, ground

Directions:

1. Grease your slow cooker with the cooking spray, add the oats, the pumpkin puree, water, milk, stevia, cinnamon, cloves, allspice, ginger and nutmeg, cover and cook on Low for 9 hours.
2. Stir the oatmeal, divide it into bowls and serve.

Nutritional Value: Calories 200; Fat 1.5g; Carbohydrates 25.5g; Protein 4g

Recipe 26: Spinach Frittata

Serving Size: 6

Cooking Time: 2 hours

Ingredients:

- 1 tablespoon olive oil
- 1 yellow onion, chopped
- 1 cup mozzarella cheese, shredded
- 3 egg whites
- 3 eggs
- 2 tablespoons milk
- Salt and black pepper to the taste
- 1 cup baby spinach
- 1 tomato, chopped

Directions:

1. Grease your Slow cooker with the oil and spread onion, spinach and tomatoes on the bottom.
2. In a bowl, mix the eggs with egg whites, milk, salt and pepper, whisk well and pour over the veggies from the pot.
3. Sprinkle mozzarella all over, cover slow cooker, cook on Low for 2 hours, slice, divide between plates and serve for breakfast.

Nutritional Value: Calories 200; Fat 8g; Carbohydrates 5g; Protein 12g

Recipe 27: Sweet Morning Chocolate Rice Pudding

Serving Size: 2

Cooking Time: 5 hours

Ingredients:

- ¾ cup evaporated milk
- ½ cup unsweetened cocoa powder
- 4 ½ cups water
- ⅔ cup packed brown sugar
- ½ cup long grain rice, uncooked

Directions:

1. Set aside evaporated milk.
2. Place the remaining ingredients in the slow cooker.
3. Whisk until well-blended.
4. Cook covered for 5-6 hours on LOW or 2-3 hours on HIGH.
5. Serve hot or cold with evaporated milk poured on top.

Nutritional Value: Calories 195; Fat 7.6g; Carbohydrates 30g; Protein 4.3g

Recipe 28: Sweet Potato Sausage Pie

Serving Size: 2

Cooking Time: 8 hours

Ingredients:

- 4 eggs, whisked
- ½ sweet potato, shredded
- ½ pound pork sausage, sliced
- ½ yellow onion, chopped
- ½ tablespoon garlic powder
- 1 teaspoon basil, dried
- A pinch of salt and black pepper
- Cooking spray

Directions:

1. Grease your slow cooker with cooking spray, add potato, sausage, onion, garlic powder, basil, salt and pepper and toss.
2. Add whisked eggs, toss everything, cover and cook on Low for 8 hours.
3. Divide between plates and serve right away for breakfast.
4. Enjoy!

Nutritional Value: Calories 271; Fat 7g; Carbohydrates 20g; Protein 11g

Recipe 29: Veggie Casserole

Serving Size: 8

Cooking Time: 4 hours

Ingredients:

- 4 egg whites
- 8 eggs
- Salt and black pepper to the taste
- 2 teaspoons ground mustard
- ¾ cup milk
- 30 ounces hash browns
- 4 bacon strips, cooked and chopped
- 1 broccoli head, chopped
- 2 bell peppers, chopped
- Cooking spray
- 6 ounces cheddar cheese, shredded
- 1 small onion, chopped

Directions:

1. In a large-sized bowl, mix the egg white with eggs, salt, pepper, mustard and milk and whisk really well.
2. Grease your Slow cooker with the spray, add hash browns, broccoli, bell peppers and onion.
3. Pour eggs mix, sprinkle bacon and cheddar on top, cover and cook on Low for 4 hours.
4. Divide between plates and serve hot for breakfast.

Nutritional Value: Calories 300; Fat 4g; Carbohydrates 18g; Protein 8g

Recipe 30: Zucchini Frittata

Serving Size: 2

Cooking Time: 3 hours

Ingredients:

- Cooking spray
- 2 eggs
- 1 zucchini, grated
- ¼ teaspoon sweet paprika
- ¼ teaspoon thyme, dried
- A pinch of salt and black pepper
- 1 and ½ tablespoon parsley, chopped
- 1 tablespoon feta cheese, crumbled
- 4 cherry tomatoes, halved

Directions:

1. In a bowl, mix eggs with zucchini, paprika, thyme, salt, pepper, cheese, parsley and tomatoes and whisk.
2. Grease your slow cooker with cooking spray, pour frittata mix, cover and cook on Low for 3 hours.
3. Divide between plates and serve for breakfast.
4. Enjoy!

Nutritional Value: Calories 261; Fat 5g; Carbohydrates 19g; Protein 6g

Chapter 3:   Lunch Recipes

Recipe 31: Apricot Barbecue Wings

Serving Size: 6

Cooking Time: 30 minutes

Ingredients:

- 4 lbs. of chicken wings, frozen
- 2 cups of BBQ sauce, bottled
- 1 cup of preserves, apricot
- 1 tablespoon of garlic powder
- 1 teaspoon of ginger powder
- 2 tablespoon of Worcestershire sauce, reduced sodium

Directions:

1. In medium-sized bowl, combine sauces and spices. Then, remove 1/2 cup of mixture and place in refrigerator.
2. Add wings to slow cooker. Cover with remaining sauce mixture. Stir till wings are coated well. Cook on the HIGH setting for three to four hours.
3. When done, set the oven to broil. Line cookie sheet using foil.
4. Remove the wings from your slow cooker. Place on cookie sheet. Drizzle with some sauce from slow cooker, if you like. Broil for about two minutes.
5. Remove cookie sheet from the oven. Flip the wings. Brush with remainder of sauce mixture from refrigerator.
6. Return wings to the oven. Broil for three to five more minutes, till the sauce has started caramelizing. Remove from the oven. Serve.

Nutritional Value: Calories 207; Fat 1.5g; Carbohydrates 25.5g; Protein 4g

Recipe 32: Apricot-Glazed Pork Roast

Serving Size: 6

Cooking Time: 6 hours

Ingredients:

- 1 medium onion, chopped
- 1 tablespoon Dijon mustard
- 1 cup apricot preserves
- ¾ cup chicken broth
- 2 pounds boneless pork loin roast
- Salt and pepper
- Cooking spray

Directions:

1. In a medium-sized bowl, mix broth, mustard, and onion.
2. Place roast in slow cooker.
3. Pour broth mixture over meat.
4. Cover and cook on LOW for 5-6 hours, until tender.

Nutritional Value: Calories 298; Fat 15.5g; Carbohydrates 9.5g; Protein 33g

Recipe 33: Barbecue Pulled Chicken

Serving Size: 4

Cooking Time: 6 hours 30 minutes

Ingredients:

- 1 teaspoon of mustard
- 2 teaspoons of lemon juice
- 1 garlic clove, minced
- ¼ cup of honey
- 1 tablespoon of tomato ketchup
- 8 ounces of skinless chicken breast fillets

Directions:

1. To make the marinade: mix the mustard, lemon juice, garlic, honey, and tomato ketchup together in a small bowl.
2. Coat the chicken fillets with the marinade and arrange them in the slow cooker pot, including any excess sauce.
3. Pour over 1/2 cup of water to allow the chicken to steam.
4. Set the slow cooker to LOW for 6 ½ hours.
5. When the cooking time is completed, shred the chicken with two forks, place back in the slow cooker and cook for 30 more minutes.
6. Serve the pulled chicken with your choice of brown bread roll and side salad.

Nutritional Value: Calories 450; Fat 3g; Carbohydrates 10g; Protein 21g

Recipe 34: Barbecue Turkey Rolls

Serving Size: 16

Cooking Time: 2 hours

Ingredients:

- Cooking oil
- 3/4 cup onions, chopped
- 3 garlic cloves, minced
- 1 lb. lean ground turkey
- 1/3 cup barbecue sauce
- 1/4 teaspoon black pepper
- 14 oz. canned tomatoes,
- 1/2 cucumber, seeded and chopped
- 16 whole-wheat pita rounds

Directions:

1. Spray skillet with cooking oil.
2. Sauté the onion and garlic.
3. Brown the turkey over medium heat. Drain oil. Add barbecue sauce, pepper, and tomatoes. Transfer to a slow cooker. Cook on the warm setting for 2 hours.
4. Spread a layer of turkey mixture and cucumber inside a pita round.
5. Roll and repeat with the remaining pita rounds. Serve and enjoy!

Nutritional Value: Calories 228; Fat 10g; Carbohydrates 18g; Protein 24g

Recipe 35: Beans and Rice

Serving Size: 6

Cooking Time: 3 hours

Ingredients:

- 1 pound pinto beans, dried
- 1/3 cup hot sauce
- Salt and black pepper to the taste
- 1 tablespoon garlic, minced
- 1 teaspoon garlic powder
- ½ teaspoon cumin, ground
- 1 tablespoon chili powder
- 3 bay leaves
- ½ teaspoon oregano, dried
- 1 cup white rice, cooked

Directions:

1. In your slow cooker, mix pinto beans with hot sauce, salt, pepper, garlic, garlic powder, cumin, chili powder, bay leaves and oregano, stir, cover and cook on High for 3 hours.
2. Divide rice between plates, add pinto beans on top and serve for lunch.

Nutritional Value: Calories 381; Fat 7g; Carbohydrates 35g; Protein 10g

Recipe 36: Beef Brisket in Orange Juice

Serving Size: 4

Cooking Time: 5 hours

Ingredients:

- 1 cup of orange juice
- 2 cups of water
- 2 tablespoons butter
- 12 oz beef brisket
- ½ teaspoon salt

Directions:

1. Toss butter in the skillet and melt.
2. Put the beef brisket in the melted butter and roast on high heat for 3 minutes per side.
3. Then sprinkle the meat with salt and transfer in the Slow Cooker.
4. Add orange juice and water.
5. Close the lid and cook the meat on High for 5 hours.

Nutritional Value: Calories 237; Fat 11.2g; Carbohydrates 6.5g; Protein 26.3g

Recipe 37: Beef Onions

Serving Size: 6

Cooking Time: 6 hours 5 minutes

Ingredients:

- 3 pounds beef roast, trimmed and boneless
- 1 tablespoon Italian seasoning
- Salt and black pepper to the taste
- 1 garlic clove, minced
- 1/3 cup sun-dried tomatoes, chopped
- ½ cup beef stock
- ½ cup kalamata olives pitted and halved
- 1 cup yellow onions chopped
- 1 tablespoon olive oil

Directions:

1. Heat up a pan with the oil over medium-high heat, add beef, brown for 5 minutes, season with black pepper and Italian seasoning, transfer to your slow cooker, add tomatoes, onions and stock, cover and cook on Low for 6 hours.
2. Transfer meat to a cutting board, slice, divide between plates, add onions and tomatoes on the side and serve with cooking juices on top.

Nutritional Value: Calories 300; Fat 5g; Carbohydrates 12g; Protein 25g

Recipe 38: Butter Chicken

Serving Size: 4

Cooking Time: 4 hours

Ingredients:

- 12 oz chicken fillet
- ½ cup butter
- 1 teaspoon garlic powder
- 1 teaspoon salt

Directions:

1. Put all ingredients in the Slow Cooker.
2. Cook them on High for 4 hours.
3. Then shred the chicken and transfer in the plates.
4. Sprinkle the chicken with fragrant butter from the Slow Cooker.

Nutritional Value: Calories 367; Fat 29.3g; Carbohydrates 0.5g; Protein 25g

Recipe 39: Cheesy Sausage Casserole

Serving Size: 4

Cooking Time: 4 hours

Ingredients:

- 2 tablespoons olive oil
- 2 pounds Italian pork sausage, chopped
- 1 onion, sliced
- 4 sun-dried tomatoes, thinly sliced
- Salt and black pepper to the taste
- ½ pound Gouda cheese, grated
- 3 yellow bell peppers, chopped
- 3 orange bell peppers, chopped
- A pinch of red pepper flakes
- 1 tablespoon parsley, chopped

Directions:

1. Heat up a pan with the oil over medium-high heat, add sausage slices, stir, cook for 3 minutes on each side and transfer to your Slow cooker.
2. Add onion, tomatoes, salt, pepper, orange bell pepper, red bell pepper, pepper flakes and sprinkle Gouda cheese at the end.
3. Cover slow cooker, cook on High for 4 hours, sprinkle parsley on top, divide between plates and serve.

Nutritional Value: Calories 260; Fat 5g; Carbohydrates 16g; Protein 14g

Recipe 40: Chicken Teriyaki

Serving Size: 4

Cooking Time: 8 hours

Ingredients:

- ½ cup chicken broth
- 1 cup teriyaki sauce
- 5 boneless chicken breasts, cut into strips
- 2 8-oz cans crushed pineapple with juice
- 3 tablespoons soy sauce
- Cooking spray
- Salt and pepper

Directions:

1. Spray slow cooker's bottom and sides with cooking spray.
2. Place chicken in slow cooker. Season generously with salt and pepper.
3. Mix together in a bowl, the teriyaki sauce, crushed pineapple with juice, and soya sauce. Pour over chicken.
4. Cover and cook on LOW for 7-8 hours.
5. Serve.

Nutritional Value: Calories 288; Fat 32g; Carbohydrates 19.1g; Protein 39g

Recipe 41: Coriander Pork and Chickpeas Stew

Serving Size: 3

Cooking Time: 8 hours 30 minutes

Ingredients:

- ½ cup beef stock
- 1 tablespoon ginger, grated
- 1 teaspoon coriander, ground
- 2 teaspoons cumin, ground
- Salt and black pepper to the taste
- 2 and ½ pounds pork stew meat, cubed
- 28 ounces canned tomatoes, drained and chopped
- 1 red onion, chopped
- 4 garlic cloves, minced
- ½ cup apricots, cut into quarters
- 15 ounces canned chickpeas, drained
- 1 tablespoon cilantro, chopped

Directions:

1. In your slow cooker, combine the meat with the stock, ginger and the rest of the ingredients except the cilantro and the chickpeas, put the lid on and cook on Low for 7 hours and 40 minutes.
2. Add the cilantro and the chickpeas, cook the stew on Low for 20 minutes more, divide into bowls and serve.

Nutritional Value: Calories 283; Fat 11.9g; Carbohydrates 28.8g; Protein 25.4g

Recipe 42: Creamy Sea Bass

Serving Size: 2

Cooking Time: 1 hour 30 minutes

Ingredients:

- 1 pound sea bass
- 2 scallion stalks, chopped
- 1 small ginger piece, grated
- 1 tablespoon soy sauce
- 2 cups coconut cream
- 4 bok choy stalks, chopped
- 3 jalapeno peppers, chopped
- Salt and black pepper to the taste

Directions:

1. Put the cream in your Slow cooker, add ginger, soy sauce, scallions, a pinch of salt, black pepper, jalapenos, stir, top with the fish and bok choy, cover and cook on High for 1 hour and 30 minutes.
2. Divide the fish mix between plates and serve.

Nutritional Value: Calories 270; Fat 3g; Carbohydrates 18g; Protein 17g

Recipe 43: Creamy Spinach and Artichoke Chicken

Serving Size: 4

Cooking Time: 4 hours

Ingredients:

- 4 ounces cream cheese
- 4 chicken breasts, boneless and skinless
- 10 ounces canned artichoke hearts, chopped
- 10 ounces spinach
- ½ cup parmesan, grated
- 1 tablespoon dried onion
- 1 tablespoon garlic, dried
- Salt and black pepper to the taste
- 4 ounces mozzarella, shredded

Directions:

1. Place chicken breasts in your Slow cooker season with salt and pepper, add artichokes, cream cheese, spinach, onion, garlic, spinach and top with mozzarella.
2. Cover slow cooker, cook on High for 4 hours, toss, divide everything between plates and serve.

Nutritional Value: Calories 450; Fat 23g; Carbohydrates 14g; Protein 39g

Recipe 44: Flank Steak with Arugula

Serving Size: 4

Cooking Time: 10 hours

Ingredients:

- 1-pound flank steak
- 1 teaspoon Worcestershire sauce
- Salt and pepper to taste
- 1 package arugula salad mix
- 2 tablespoon balsamic vinegar

Directions:

1. Season the flank steak with Worcestershire sauce, salt, and pepper.
2. Place in the crockpot that has been lined with aluminum foil.
3. Close the cover lid and cook on low for 10 hours or on high for 7 hours.
4. Meanwhile, prepare the salad by combining the arugula salad mix and balsamic vinegar. Set aside in the fridge.
5. Once the steak is cooked, allow to cool before slicing.
6. Serve on top of the arugula salad.

Nutritional Value: Calories 452; Fat 29.5g; Carbohydrates 5.8g; Protein 30.2g

Recipe 45: Garlic-Infused Turkey Breast

Serving Size: 6

Cooking Time: 10 hours

Ingredients:

- 2 quartered medium onions
- 2 heads of garlic cloves
- ½ cup water
- 1 bone-in turkey breast, about 5-6 pounds
- Salt and pepper to taste
- 2 tablespoons butter, at room temperature

Directions:

1. Prepare garlic by peeling the cloves. There should be around 20 cloves. Smash about half of the cloves with a large blade. Set aside.
2. Rinse turkey thoroughly under running water, and pat dry with paper towels.
3. Sprinkle turkey with salt and pepper. Rub the butter all over the turkey's skin and under the skin.
4. Place smashed garlic in the turkey breast cavity.
5. Place in slow cooker. Add water on the side of the slow cooker to cover the bottom.
6. Add onion and remaining garlic around the side of cooker and cover.
7. Cook on LOW for 9-10 hours.
8. Remove from slow cooker, and let stand for 15 minutes before slicing.

Nutritional Value: Calories 359; Fat 39.8g; Carbohydrates 6.6g; Protein 82g

Recipe 46: Honey Beef Sausages

Serving Size: 4

Cooking Time: 4 hours 30 minutes

Ingredients:

- 1-pound beef sausages
- 2 tablespoons of liquid honey
- 1 teaspoon dried dill
- ½ teaspoon salt
- ¼ cup heavy cream

Directions:

1. In the mixing bowl mix liquid honey with dried dill and salt.
2. Then add cream and whisk until smooth.
3. Pour the liquid in the Slow Cooker.
4. Add beef sausages and close the lid.
5. Cook the meal on High for 4.5 hours.

Nutritional Value: Calories 507; Fat 43.9g; Carbohydrates 12.1g; Protein 15.9g

Recipe 47: Lamb Casserole

Serving Size: 2

Cooking Time: 7 hours

Ingredients:

- 2 garlic cloves, minced
- 1 red onion, chopped
- 1 tablespoon olive oil
- 1 celery stick, chopped
- 10 ounces lamb fillet, cut into medium pieces
- Salt and black pepper to the taste
- 1 and ¼ cups lamb stock
- 2 carrots, chopped
- ½ tablespoon rosemary, chopped
- 1 leek, chopped
- 1 tablespoon mint sauce
- 1 teaspoon sugar
- 1 tablespoon tomato puree
- ½ cauliflower, florets separated
- ½ celeriac, chopped
- 2 tablespoons butter

Directions:

1. Heat up a slow cooker with the oil over medium heat, add garlic, onion and celery, stir and cook for 5 minutes.
2. Add lamb pieces, stir, brown for 3 minutes and transfer everything to your Slow cooker.
3. Add carrot, leek, rosemary, stock, tomato puree, mint sauce, sugar, cauliflower, celeriac, butter, salt and black pepper, cover and cook on Low for 7 hours.
4. Divide lamb and all the veggies between plates and serve.

Nutritional Value: Calories 324; Fat 4g; Carbohydrates 12g; Protein 20g

Recipe 48: Lemon Garlic Dump Chicken

Serving Size: 6

Cooking Time: 8 hours

Ingredients:

- ¼ cup olive oil
- 2 teaspoon garlic, minced
- 6 chicken breasts, bones removed
- 1 tablespoon parsley, chopped
- 2 tablespoons lemon juice, freshly squeezed

Directions:

1. Heat oil in a large-sized skillet over medium flame.
2. Sauté the garlic until golden brown.
3. Arrange the chicken breasts in the crockpot.
4. Pour over the oil with garlic.
5. Add the parsley and lemon juice. Add a little water.
6. Close the cover lid and cook on low for 8 hours or on high for 6 hours.

Nutritional Value: Calories 581; Fat 35.8g; Carbohydrates 0.7g; Protein 60.5g

Recipe 49: Orange Beef Dish

Serving Size: 5

Cooking Time: 5 hours

Ingredients:

- 1 pound beef sirloin steak, cut into medium strips
- 2 and ½ cups shiitake mushrooms, sliced
- 1 yellow onion, cut into medium wedges
- 3 red hot chilies, dried
- ¼ cup brown sugar
- ¼ cup orange juice
- ¼ cup soy sauce
- 2 tablespoons cider vinegar
- 1 tablespoon cornstarch
- 1 tablespoon ginger, grated
- 1 tablespoon sesame oil
- 1 cup snow peas
- 2 garlic cloves, minced
- 1 tablespoon orange zest, grated

Directions:

1. In your Slow cooker, mix steak strips with mushrooms, onion, chilies, sugar, orange juice, soy sauce, vinegar, cornstarch, ginger, oil, garlic and orange zest, toss, cover and cook on Low for 4 hours and 30 minutes.
2. Add snow peas, cover, cook on Low for 30 minutes more, divide between plates and serve.

Nutritional Value: Calories 310; Fat 7g; Carbohydrates 26g; Protein 33g

Recipe 50: Pepperoni Chicken

Serving Size: 6

Cooking Time: 6 hours

Ingredients:

- 14 ounces pizza sauce
- 1 tablespoon olive oil
- 4 medium chicken breasts, skinless and boneless
- Salt and black pepper to the taste
- 1 teaspoon oregano, dried
- 6 ounces mozzarella, sliced
- 1 teaspoon garlic powder
- 2 ounces pepperoni, sliced

Directions:

1. Put the chicken in your Slow cooker, add pizza sauce, oil, salt, pepper, garlic powder, pepperoni and mozzarella, cover and cook on Low for 6 hours.
2. Toss everything, divide between plates and serve.

Nutritional Value: Calories 320; Fat 10g; Carbohydrates 14g; Protein 27g

Recipe 51: Pork Belly and Applesauce

Serving Size: 6

Cooking Time: 8 hours

Ingredients:

- 2 tablespoons sugar
- 1 tablespoon lemon juice
- 1 quart water
- 17 ounces apples, cored and cut into wedges
- 2 pounds pork belly, scored
- Salt and black pepper to the taste
- A drizzle of olive oil

Directions:

1. In your blender, mix water with apples, lemon juice and sugar and pulse well
2. Put the pork belly in your Slow cooker, add oil, salt, pepper and applesauce, toss, cover and cook on Low for 8 hours.
3. Slice pork roast, divide between plates and serve with the applesauce on top.

Nutritional Value: Calories 456; Fat 34g; Carbohydrates 10g; Protein 25g

Recipe 52: Ranch Seasoned Beef

Serving Size: 4

Cooking Time: 8 hours

Ingredients:

- 1 packet ranch seasoning for salad such as Hidden Valley Ranch Packet
- 3 lbs beef chuck pot roast, boneless and cut into large cubes
- Cooking Spray
- 3 garlic cloves, minced
- ½ cup water
- 1/3 cup white vinegar
- 1 large sweet onion, sliced
- Salt and pepper

Directions:

1. Spray crock pot with cooking spray.
2. Season the beef with salt and pepper. Place beef in the slow cooker.
3. Add sliced onions.
4. Mix ranch packet, garlic, water, and vinegar. Pour on beef.
5. Cook on LOW for 8 hours.

Nutritional Value: Calories 322; Fat 30g; Carbohydrates 28g; Protein 14g

Recipe 53: Salsa Chicken

Serving Size: 4

Cooking Time: 7 hours

Ingredients:

- 4 chicken breasts, skinless and boneless
- ½ cup veggie stock
- Salt and black pepper to the taste
- 16 ounces salsa
- 1 and ½ tablespoons parsley, dried
- 1 teaspoon garlic powder
- ½ tablespoon cilantro, chopped
- 1 teaspoon onion powder
- ½ tablespoons oregano, dried
- ½ teaspoon paprika, smoked
- 1 teaspoon chili powder
- ½ teaspoon cumin, ground

Directions:

1. Put the stock in your slow cooker, add chicken breasts, add salsa, parsley, garlic powder, cilantro, onion powder, oregano, paprika, chili powder, cumin, salt and black pepper to the taste, stir, cover and cook on Low for 7 hours.
2. Divide chicken between plates, drizzle the sauces on top and serve for lunch.

Nutritional Value: Calories 270; Fat 4g; Carbohydrates 14g; Protein 9g

Recipe 54: Saucy Chopped Steaks

Serving Size: 4

Cooking Time: 8 hours

Ingredients:

- 1 (10¾-ounce) can cream of mushroom soup
- 4 chopped steaks
- 1 large onion, chopped
- 2 carrots, peeled, cut into 1-inch slices

Directions:

1. Place half of the soup into slow cooker; spread evenly across bottom.
2. Place steaks side-by-side in slow cooker; spoon remaining soup evenly over top of steaks.
3. Place onions and carrots on top.
4. Cook on Low for approximately about 8 hours, or until tender.

Nutritional Value: Calories 456; Fat 2.9g; Carbohydrates 7.1g; Protein 1.2g

Recipe 55: Soy-Ginger Steamed Pompano

Serving Size: 6

Cooking Time: 50 minutes

Ingredients:

- 1 wild-caught whole pompano, gutted and scaled
- 1 bunch scallion, diced
- 1 bunch cilantro, chopped
- 3 teaspoons minced garlic
- 1 tablespoon grated ginger
- 1 tablespoon swerve sweetener
- ¼ cup soy sauce
- ¼ cup white wine
- ¼ cup sesame oil

Directions:

1. Place scallions in a 6-quart slow cooker and top with fish.
2. Whisk together the remaining ingredients, except for cilantro, and pour the mixture all over the fish.
3. Plug in the slow cooker, shut with lid, and cook for 1 hour at a high heat setting or until cooked through.
4. Garnish with cilantro and serve.

Nutritional Value: Calories 283; Fat 11.9g; Carbohydrates 28.8g; Protein 25.4g

Recipe 56: Sweet and Sour Chicken Wings

Serving Size: 32

Cooking Time: 3 hours

Ingredients:

- 1 cup sugar
- 1 cup cider vinegar
- 1/2 cup ketchup
- 2 tablespoons reduced-sodium soy sauce
- 1 teaspoon chicken bouillon granules
- 16 chicken wings
- 3 tablespoons cornstarch
- 1/2 cup cold water

Directions:

1. Mix the first 5 ingredients in a small saucepan. Boil it, stir and cook until the sugar dissolves.
2. In the meantime, slice through the 2 joints of the wings with a sharp knife; dispose of the wingtips. Remove the wings to a 5-quart slow cooker, pour in the sugar mixture. Cook on low for 3 to 3 1/2 hours, or until the chicken juices run clear.
3. Transfer the wings to a heated serving dish. Remove the fat from the cooking juices; remove to a small saucepan. Boil the liquid. Mix water and cornstarch until smooth. Slowly mix into the pan. Boil it, stir and cook for 2 minutes until thickened. Add to the chicken. Enjoy with a slotted spoon.

Nutritional Value: Calories 260; Fat 11g; Carbohydrates 5g; Protein 20g

Recipe 57: Tender Pork Chops

Serving Size: 4

Cooking Time: 8 hours

Ingredients:

- 2 yellow onions, chopped
- 6 bacon slices, chopped
- ½ cup chicken stock
- Salt and black pepper to the taste
- 4 pork chops

Directions:

1. In your Slow cooker, mix onions with bacon, stock, salt, pepper and pork chops, cover and cook on Low for 8 hours.
2. Divide pork chops on plates, drizzle cooking juices all over and serve.

Nutritional Value: Calories 325; Fat 18g; Carbohydrates 12g; Protein 36g

Recipe 58: Thyme Beef

Serving Size: 2

Cooking Time: 5 hours

Ingredients:

- 8 oz beef sirloin, chopped
- 1 tablespoon dried thyme
- 1 tablespoon olive oil
- ½ cup of water
- 1 teaspoon salt

Directions:

1. Preheat the skillet well.
2. Then mix beef with dried thyme and olive oil.
3. Put the meat in the hot skillet and roast for 2 minutes per side on high heat.
4. Then transfer the meat in the Slow Cooker.
5. Add salt and water.
6. Cook the meal on High for 5 hours.

Nutritional Value: Calories 274; Fat 14.2g; Carbohydrates 0.9g; Protein 34.5g

Recipe 59: Tomato Chicken Sausages

Serving Size: 4

Cooking Time: 2 hours

Ingredients:

- 1-pound chicken sausages
- 1 cup tomato juice
- 1 tablespoon dried sage
- 1 teaspoon salt
- 1 teaspoon olive oil

Directions:

1. Heat the olive oil in the skillet well.
2. Add chicken sausages and roast them for 1 minute per side on high heat.
3. Then transfer the chicken sausages in the Slow Cooker.
4. Add all remaining ingredients and close the lid.
5. Cook the chicken sausages on High for 2 hours.

Nutritional Value: Calories 236; Fat 13.7g; Carbohydrates 10.5g; Protein 15.3g

Recipe 60: Tropical-Flavored Chicken

Serving Size: 6

Cooking Time: 6 hours

Ingredients:

- 3 medium-sized sweet potatoes
- 1 whole large chicken, cut in pieces
- 1 20-oz can pineapple chunks, in juice
- 2 cups can chicken broth
- 2 tablespoons cornstarch
- 2 tablespoons cold water

Directions:

1. Wash, peel, and cube sweet potatoes.
2. Place cut-up chicken in slow cooker.
3. Place the sweet potatoes over the chicken in the slow cooker.
4. Pour chicken broth in the slow cooker.
5. Add the pineapples and juice on top.
6. Cover and cook on LOW for 6 hours, or until chicken and potatoes are tender.
7. Mix cornstarch and water until smooth just before serving. Stir cornstarch paste into cooker. Cook for approximately about an additional 8-10 minutes, until sauce thickens.

Nutritional Value: Calories 517; Fat 8.5g; Carbohydrates 40g; Protein 67g

Chapter 4:   Dinner Recipes

Recipe 61: Almond-Crusted Tilapia

Serving Size: 4

Cooking Time: 4 hours

Ingredients:

- 2 tablespoons olive oil
- 1 cup chopped almonds
- ¼ cup ground flaxseed
- 4 tilapia fillets
- Salt and pepper to taste

Directions:

1. Line the bottom of the crockpot with a foil.
2. Grease the foil with the olive oil.
3. In a mixing bowl, combine the almonds and flaxseed.
4. Season the tilapia with salt and pepper to taste.
5. Dredge the tilapia fillets with the almond and flaxseed mixture.
6. Place neatly in the foil-lined crockpot.
7. Close the cover lid and cook on high for 2 hours and on low for 4 hours.

Nutritional Value: Calories 233; Fat 13.3g; Carbohydrates 4.6g; Protein 25.5g

Recipe 62: Balsamic Chicken Thighs

Serving Size: 8

Cooking Time: 4 hours

Ingredients:

- 1 teaspoon garlic powder
- 1 teaspoon dried basil
- 1/2 teaspoon salt
- 1/2 teaspoon pepper
- 2 teaspoons dehydrated onion
- 4 garlic cloves minced
- 1 tablespoon extra-virgin olive oil
- 1/2 cup balsamic vinegar divided
- 8 chicken thighs boneless, skinless
- sprinkle of fresh chopped parsley

Directions:

1. In a small dish, combine the first five dry spices and distribute them evenly over both sides of the chicken. Remove from the equation.
2. Pour olive oil and garlic on the bottom of the slow-cooker. Pour in 1/4 cup balsamic vinegar—place chicken on top.
3. Sprinkle remaining balsamic vinegar over the chicken. If you have a new slow cooker, cover and cook on high for 3 hours. You may need to cook for an additional hour if you have an older slow cooker. Serve with a garnish of fresh parsley.

Nutritional Value: Calories 217; Fat 16.3g; Carbohydrates 3.4g; Protein 14.7g

Recipe 63: Buffalo Ranch Slow Cooker Chicken Wings

Serving Size: 8

Cooking Time: 3 hours

Ingredients:

- 2 pounds of chicken wings, bone-in
- 1 cup of wing sauce, buffalo flavor
- 1 packet of Ranch salad dressing
- Salt, kosher
- Pepper, ground

Directions:

1. Place the wings in your slow cooker.
2. In large mixing bowl, combine buffalo sauce with ranch seasoning. Season as desired. Pour the mixture over the wings, Coat by stirring.
3. Cover slow cooker. Cook on the HIGH setting till cooked fully through, between 2 & 3 hours.
4. Heat the oven broiler. Line two cookie sheets with baking paper. Lay wings on them. Place pans under broiler till wings are crispy, five minutes or so. Serve.

Nutritional Value: Calories 283; Fat 11.9g; Carbohydrates 28.8g; Protein 25.4g

Recipe 64: Chili Catfish

Serving Size: 4

Cooking Time: 6 hours

Ingredients:

- 1 catfish, boneless and cut into 4 pieces
- 3 red chili peppers, chopped
- ½ cup sugar
- ¼ cup water
- 1 tablespoon soy sauce
- 1 shallot, minced
- A small ginger piece, grated
- 1 tablespoon coriander, chopped

Directions:

1. Put catfish pieces in your Slow cooker.
2. Heat up a pan with the coconut sugar over medium-high heat and stir until it caramelizes.
3. Add soy sauce, shallot, ginger, water and chili pepper, stir, pour over the fish, add coriander, cover and cook on Low for 6 hours.
4. Divide fish between plates and serve with the sauce from the slow cooker drizzled on top.

Nutritional Value: Calories 200; Fat 4g; Carbohydrates 8g; Protein 10g

Recipe 65: Chipotle Shredded Pork

Serving Size: 8

Cooking Time: 6 hours

Ingredients:

- 1 (7.5-ounce) can chipotle peppers in adobo sauce
- 1 ½ tablespoons of apple cider vinegar
- 1 tablespoon of ground cumin
- 1 tablespoon of dried oregano
- Juice of 1 lime
- 2 pounds of pork shoulder, trimmed of excess fat

Directions:

1. Puree the chipotle peppers and adobo sauce using the blender, apple cider vinegar, cumin, oregano, and lime juice.
2. Place the prepared pork shoulder in the slow cooker, and pour the sauce over it.
3. Cover the slow cooker, and cook on low for 6 hours.
4. The finished pork should shred easily. Use two forks to actually shred the pork in the slow cooker. If there is any additional sauce, allow the pork to cook on low for 20 minutes more to absorb the remaining liquid.

Nutritional Value: Calories 260; Fat 11g; Carbohydrates 5g; Protein 20g

Recipe 66: Cod with Asparagus

Serving Size: 4

Cooking Time: 2 hours

Ingredients:

- 4 cod fillets, boneless
- 1 bunch asparagus
- 12 tablespoon lemon juice
- Salt and black pepper to the taste
- 2 tablespoon olive oil

Directions:

1. Place the cod fillets in separate foil sheets.
2. Top the fish with asparagus spears, lemon pepper, oil, and lemon juice.
3. Wrap the fish with its foil sheet then place them in Slow Cooker.
4. Put the cooker's lid on and set the cooking time to 2 hours on High settings.
5. Unwrap the fish and serve warm.

Nutritional Value: Calories 202; Fat 3g; Carbohydrates 7g; Protein 3g

Recipe 67: Creamy Vegetable Curry

Serving Size: 6

Cooking Time: 7 hours and 30 minutes

Ingredients:

- 2 cups fresh mushrooms
- 2 cups asparagus, trimmed and steamed
- 6 red potatoes, sliced into cubes
- 2 cups baby carrots
- 5 green onions, minced
- 1 ½ cups green peas
- 1 ½ cups corn kernels
- 2 tablespoons curry powder
- 30 ounces curry sauce
- 1 ½ teaspoons ground mustard
- 2 teaspoons garam masala
- ¼ cup fresh parsley, chopped

For serving

- Hot cooked rice
- Naan flatbreads

Directions:

1. Add the fresh mushrooms, asparagus, potatoes, carrots, green onions, green peas and corn kernels to your slow cooker.
2. Toss to combine.
3. In a bowl, mix the curry powder, curry sauce, ground mustard, and garam masala.
4. Add this mixture to the pot.
5. Cover the pot. Cook on low for 7 hours.
6. Sprinkle with the parsley.
7. Serve with the rice or naan flatbread.

Nutritional Value: Calories 228; Fat 10g; Carbohydrates 18g; Protein 24g

Recipe 68: Fish and Tomatoes

Serving Size: 4

Cooking Time: 1 hour 30 minutes

Ingredients:

- 1 pound cod fillets, skinless and boneless
- 1 yellow onion, chopped
- 1 red bell pepper, chopped
- 3 garlic cloves, minced
- 15 ounces canned tomatoes, chopped
- 1 tablespoons rosemary, chopped
- ¼ cup veggie stock
- A pinch of red pepper flakes, crushed
- A pinch of salt and black pepper

Directions:

1. In your slow cooker, mix tomatoes with onion, bell pepper, garlic, rosemary, stock, pepper flakes, salt and pepper and stir.
2. Add fish fillets on top, cover and cook on Low for 1 hour and 30 minutes.
3. Divide everything between plates and serve.
4. Enjoy!

Nutritional Value: Calories 200; Fat 4g; Carbohydrates 7g; Protein 4g

Recipe 69: Flavored Tilapia

Serving Size: 4

Cooking Time: 2 hours

Ingredients:

- 1 asparagus bunch, spears trimmed
- 12 tablespoons lemon juice
- 4 tilapia fillets
- A pinch of lemon pepper
- 2 tablespoons olive oil

Directions:

1. Divide tilapia fillets on 4 parchment paper pieces.
2. Divide asparagus on top, drizzle the lemon juice and sprinkle a pinch of pepper.
3. Drizzle the oil all over, wrap fish and asparagus and place in your slow cooker.
4. Cover and cook on High for 2 hours.
5. Unwrap fish, divide between plates and serve.
6. Enjoy!

Nutritional Value: Calories 200; Fat 3g; Carbohydrates 8g; Protein 6g

Recipe 70: Garlic Pulled Chicken

Serving Size: 4

Cooking Time: 4 hours

Ingredients:

- 1-pound chicken breast, skinless, boneless
- 1 tablespoon minced garlic
- 2 cups of water
- ½ cup plain yogurt

Directions:

1. Put the chicken breast in the Slow Cooker.
2. Add minced garlic and water.
3. Close the lid and cook the chicken on High for 4 hours.
4. Then drain water and shred the chicken breast.
5. Add plain yogurt and stir the pulled chicken well.

Nutritional Value: Calories 154; Fat 3.2g; Carbohydrates 2.9g; Protein 25.9g

Recipe 71: Ginger Ground Pork

Serving Size: 3

Cooking Time: 6 hours

Ingredients:

- 1.5 cup ground pork
- 1 oz minced ginger
- 2 tablespoons coconut oil
- 1 tablespoon tomato paste
- ½ teaspoon chili powder

Directions:

1. Mix ground pork with minced ginger, tomato paste, and chili powder.
2. Put the ground pork in the Slow Cooker.
3. Add coconut oil and close the lid.
4. Cook the meal on Low for 6 hours.

Nutritional Value: Calories 193; Fat 15.1g; Carbohydrates 7.9g; Protein 7.8g

Recipe 72: Lemon Pepper Tilapia

Serving Size: 6

Cooking Time: 40 minutes

Ingredients:

- 6 wild-caught Tilapia fillets
- 4 teaspoons lemon-pepper seasoning, divided
- 6 tablespoons unsalted butter, divided
- ½ cup lemon juice, fresh

Directions:

1. Cut a large piece of aluminum foil for each fillet and then arrange them in a clean working space.
2. Place each fillet in the middle of the foil, then season with lemon-pepper seasoning, drizzle with lemon juice, and top with 1 tablespoon butter.
3. Gently crimp the edges of foil to form a packet and place it into a 6-quart slow cooker.
4. Plug in the slow cooker, shut with lid, and cook for 3 hours at a high heat setting or until cooked through.
5. When done, carefully remove packets from the slow cooker, open the crimped edges, and check the fish; it should be tender and flaky.
6. Serve straightaway.

Nutritional Value: Calories 217; Fat 16.3g; Carbohydrates 3.4g; Protein 14.7g

Recipe 73: Mackarel and Lemon

Serving Size: 4

Cooking Time: 4 hours

Ingredients:

- 4 mackerels
- 3 ounces breadcrumbs
- Juice and rind of 1 lemon
- 1 tablespoon chives, finely chopped
- Salt and black pepper to the taste
- 1 egg, whisked
- 1 tablespoon butter
- 1 tablespoon vegetable oil
- 3 lemon wedges

Directions:

1. In a bowl, mix breadcrumbs with lemon juice, lemon rind, salt, pepper, egg and chives, stir very well and coat mackerel with this mix.
2. Add the oil and the butter to your Slow cooker and arrange mackerel inside.
3. Cover, cook on High for 2 hours, divide fish between plates and serve with lemon wedges on the side.

Nutritional Value: Calories 200; Fat 3g; Carbohydrates 3g; Protein 12g

Recipe 74: Marinara Chicken Pasta

Serving Size: 7

Cooking Time: 4 hours 10 minutes

Ingredients:

- 1 jar-24 oz. marinara vegetable pasta sauce
- 2 chicken laps, boneless and skinless
- 1 cup medium red bell pepper, chopped
- 8oz penne pasta. Cooked and drained

Directions:

1. Place chicken in a slow cooker.
2. Add the pepper and pasta sauce and cook for 4 hours.
3. When done, dish the pasta into a plate and spread the chicken sauce over it.
4. Serve and enjoy.

Nutritional Value: Calories 283; Fat 11.9g; Carbohydrates 28.8g; Protein 25.4g

Recipe 75: Mustard Pork Chops

Serving Size: 2

Cooking Time: 4 hours

Ingredients:

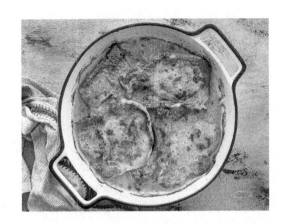

- 1 tablespoon butter
- 1 pound pork chops, bone in
- 1 tablespoon grainy mustard
- 1 tablespoon yellow mustard
- 2 tablespoons mayonnaise
- 1 tablespoon BBQ sauce
- ½ tablespoon honey
- ½ tablespoon lime juice

Directions:

1. In your slow cooker, mix butter with pork chops, grainy mustard, yellow mustard, mayonnaise, BBQ sauce, honey and lime juice, stir, cover and cook on High for 4 hours.
2. Divide pork chops and mustard sauce between plates and serve with a side salad.
3. Enjoy!

Nutritional Value: Calories 300; Fat 8g; Carbohydrates 16g; Protein 16g

Recipe 76: Old Fashioned Shredded Beef

Serving Size: 4

Cooking Time: 6 hours

Ingredients:

- ½ cup of canned soup
- 1 cup of water
- 1-pound beef tenderloin
- 1 teaspoon peppercorns

Directions:

1. Pour water in the Slow Cooker.
2. Add peppercorns and beef tenderloin.
3. Close the lid and cook the meat on High for 5 hours.
4. After this, drain water and shred the meat with the help of the forks.
5. Add canned soup and stir well.
6. Cook the beef on High for 1 hour.

Nutritional Value: Calories 247; Fat 10.9g; Carbohydrates 1.8g; Protein 33.4g

Recipe 77: Onion Pork, Beef and Greens

Serving Size: 2

Cooking Time: 8 hours

Ingredients:

- ½ pound black beans
- 1 bacon slice, chopped
- ½ pound pork shoulder, cubed
- Salt and black pepper to the taste
- ½ pound beef chuck, boneless and cut into medium cubes
- 3 garlic cloves, minced
- ½ yellow onion, chopped
- ½ cup chicken stock
- ¼ pound smoked ham hock
- ¼ tablespoon apple cider vinegar
- ½ bunch collard greens
- 1 tablespoon olive oil

Directions:

1. In your slow cooker, mix beans with bacon, pork, salt, pepper, beef, 2 garlic cloves, onion, stock and apple cider, stir, cover, cook on Low for 8 hours and divide everything between plates.
2. Heat up a pan with the oil over medium-high heat, add the rest of the garlic, stir and cook for 1 minute.
3. Add collard greens, stir, cook for a few minutes and divide next to meat and beans.
4. Serve right away.
5. Enjoy!

Nutritional Value: Calories 453; Fat 10g; Carbohydrates 20g; Protein 36g

Recipe 78: Poached Milkfish

Serving Size: 2

Cooking Time: 4 hours

Ingredients:

- 1 pound milkfish
- 6 garlic cloves, minced
- 1 small ginger pieces, chopped
- ½ tablespoon black peppercorns
- 1 cup pineapple juice
- 1 cup pineapple, chopped
- ¼ cup white vinegar
- 4 jalapeno peppers, chopped
- A pinch of sea salt
- Black pepper to the taste

Directions:

1. Put the fish in your slow cooker and season with a pinch of salt and some black pepper.
2. Add garlic, ginger, peppercorns, pineapple juice, pineapple chunks, vinegar and jalapenos.
3. Stir gently, cover and eventually cook on Low for 4 hours.
4. Divide fish between 2 plates and top with the pineapple mix.
5. Enjoy!

Nutritional Value: Calories 240; Fat 4g; Carbohydrates 8g; Protein 3g

Recipe 79: Pork Shoulder

Serving Size: 4

Cooking Time: 7 hours

Ingredients:

- 2 and ½ pounds pork shoulder
- 4 cups chicken stock
- ½ cup coconut aminos
- ¼ cup white vinegar
- 2 tablespoons chili sauce
- Juice from 1 lime
- 1 tablespoon ginger, grated
- 1 tablespoon Chinese 5 spice
- 2 cup by portabella mushrooms, sliced
- A pinch of salt and black pepper
- 1 zucchini, sliced

Directions:

1. In your slow cooker, mix pork shoulder with stock, aminos, vinegar, chili sauce, lime juice, ginger, 5 spice, mushrooms, zucchini, salt and pepper, toss a bit, cover and cook on Low for 7 hours.
2. Transfer pork shoulder to a cutting board, shred using 2 forks, return to Crockpot and toss with the rest of the ingredients.
3. Divide pork between plates and serve.
4. Enjoy!

Nutritional Value: Calories 342; Fat 6g; Carbohydrates 27g; Protein 18g

Recipe 80: Sea Bass in Coconut Cream Sauce

Serving Size: 3

Cooking Time: 1 hour

Ingredients:

- 18-ounce wild-caught sea bass
- 5 jalapeno peppers
- 4 stalks of bock Choy
- 2 stalks of scallions, sliced
- 1 tablespoon grated ginger
- 1 ½ teaspoon salt
- 1 tablespoon fish sauce, unsweetened
- 2 cups coconut cream

Directions:

1. Stir together all the ingredients except for bok choy and fish in a bowl and add this mixture to a 6-quarts slow cooker.
2. Plug in the slow cooker, add fish, top with bok choy, and shut with lid.
3. Cook sea bass for 1 hour and 30 minutes or until cooked.
4. Serve straightaway.

Nutritional Value: Calories 228; Fat 10g; Carbohydrates 18g; Protein 24g

Recipe 81: Simple Pork Meatballs in Tomato Sauce

Serving Size: 8

Cooking Time: 8 hours

Ingredients:

- 1 egg, beaten
- 1 28-oz can of tomato sauce
- 1 16-oz can crushed tomatoes
- 1 medium yellow onion, chopped
- 1½ pounds ground pork
- ½ cup water
- Salt and pepper

Directions:

1. Mix ground pork, egg, water, and onion in a medium-sized bowl.
2. Season generously with salt and pepper.
3. Shape mixture into about 20-24 meatballs.
4. Mix the crushed tomatoes and spaghetti sauce in the slow cooker.
5. Place meatballs into the sauce mixture.
6. Cook on LOW for 8 hours.

Nutritional Value: Calories 186; Fat 20.7g; Carbohydrates 14.9g; Protein 35.3g

Recipe 82: Slow Cooker Chili

Serving Size: 15

Cooking Time: 30 minutes

Ingredients:

- 2 lb. of beef, ground
- 1/2 cup of onions, chopped
- 2 minced cloves of garlic
- 2 x 16-oz. cans of rinsed, drained kidney beans, dark red
- 2 x 16-oz. cans of rinsed, drained kidney beans, light red
- 2 x 14 & 1/2-oz. cans of cut-up tomatoes, stewed
- 1 x 15-oz. can of pizza sauce
- 1 x 4-oz. can of green chilies, chopped
- 1 teaspoon of basil, dried
- 4 teaspoon of chili powder
- 1/2 teaspoon of salt, kosher
- 1/8 teaspoon of pepper, ground

Directions:

1. Brown the ground beef, garlic, and onions in a large saucepan over medium heat. Heat till no pink remains in meat. Drain well.
2. Transfer mixture to large slow cooker. Add remainder of ingredients and stir. Cover slow cooker. Cook on low setting for six hours. Serve.

Nutritional Value: Calories 207; Fat 1.5g; Carbohydrates 25.5g; Protein 4g

Recipe 83: Steak Pizzaiola

Serving Size: 4

Cooking Time: 8 hours

Ingredients:

- 1 ½ cup pasta sauce
- ¼ cup of water
- 1 medium-sized onion, sliced
- 1 bell pepper, sliced
- 1-2 lb. London broil steaks
- Salt and pepper

Directions:

1. Place all ingredients into the slow cooker.
2. Season with salt and pepper.
3. Cook on LOW for about 7-8 hours, flipping it once or twice.
4. Serve with pasta, potatoes, bread or vegetables.

Nutritional Value: Calories 273; Fat 11g; Carbohydrates 44g; Protein 24g

Recipe 84: Sweet Turkey

Serving Size: 12

Cooking Time: 3 hours 30 minutes

Ingredients:

- 14 ounces chicken stock
- ¼ cup brown sugar
- ½ cup lemon juice
- ¼ cup lime juice
- ¼ cup sage, chopped
- ¼ cup cider vinegar
- 2 tablespoons mustard
- ¼ cup olive oil
- 1 tablespoon marjoram, chopped
- 1 teaspoon sweet paprika
- Salt and black pepper to the taste
- 1 teaspoon garlic powder
- 2 turkey breast halves, boneless and skinless

Directions:

1. In your blender, mix stock with brown sugar, lemon juice, lime juice, sage, vinegar, mustard, oil, marjoram, paprika, salt, pepper and garlic powder and pulse well.
2. Put turkey breast halves in a bowl, add blender mix, cover and leave aside in the fridge for 8 hours.
3. Transfer everything to your Slow cooker, cover and cook on High for 3 hours and 30 minutes.
4. Divide between plates and serve for lunch.

Nutritional Value: Calories 219; Fat 4g; Carbohydrates 5g; Protein 36g

Recipe 85: Tabasco Halibut

Serving Size: 4

Cooking Time: 2 hours

Ingredients:

- ½ cup parmesan, grated
- ¼ cup butter, melted
- ¼ cup mayonnaise
- 2 tablespoons green onions, chopped
- 6 garlic cloves, minced
- ½ teaspoon Tabasco sauce
- 4 halibut fillets, boneless
- Salt and black pepper to the taste
- Juice of ½ lemon

Directions:

1. Season halibut with salt, pepper and some of the lemon juice, place in your Slow cooker, add butter, mayo, green onions, garlic, Tabasco sauce and lemon juice, toss a bit, cover and cook on High for 2 hours.
2. Add parmesan, leave fish mix aside for a few more minutes, divide between plates and serve.

Nutritional Value: Calories 240; Fat 12g; Carbohydrates 15g; Protein 23g

Recipe 86: Tender Duck Fillets

Serving Size: 3

Cooking Time: 8 hours

Ingredients:

- 1 tablespoon butter
- 1 teaspoon dried rosemary
- 1 teaspoon ground nutmeg
- 9 oz duck fillet
- 1 cup of water

Directions:

1. Slice the fillet.
2. Then melt the butter in the skillet.
3. Add sliced duck fillet and roast it for 2-3 minutes per side on medium heat.
4. Transfer the roasted duck fillet and butter in the Slow Cooker.
5. Add dried rosemary, ground nutmeg, and water.
6. Close the lid and cook the meal on Low for 8 hours.

Nutritional Value: Calories 145; Fat 4.7g; Carbohydrates 0.6g; Protein 25.2g

Recipe 87: Teriyaki Pork

Serving Size: 8

Cooking Time: 7 hours

Ingredients:

- 2 tablespoons sugar
- 2 tablespoons soy sauce
- ¾ cup apple juice
- 1 teaspoon ginger powder
- 1 tablespoon white vinegar
- Salt and black pepper to the taste
- ¼ teaspoon garlic powder
- 3 pounds pork loin roast, halved
- 7 teaspoons cornstarch
- 3 tablespoons water

Directions:

1. In your Slow cooker, mix apple juice with sugar, soy sauce, vinegar, ginger, garlic powder, salt, pepper and pork loin, toss well, cover and cook on Low for 7 hours.
2. Transfer cooking juices to a small pan, heat up over medium-high heat, add cornstarch mixed with water, stir well, cook for 2 minutes until it thickens and take off heat.
3. Slice roast, divide between plates, drizzle sauce all over and serve for lunch.

Nutritional Value: Calories 247; Fat 8g; Carbohydrates 9g; Protein 33g

Recipe 88: Turkey and Orange Sauce

Serving Size: 4

Cooking Time: 8 hours

Ingredients:

- 4 turkey wings
- 2 tablespoons ghee, melted
- 2 tablespoons olive oil
- 1 and ½ cups cranberries, dried
- Salt and black pepper to the taste
- 1 yellow onion, roughly chopped
- 1 cup walnuts
- 1 cup orange juice
- 1 bunch thyme, chopped

Directions:

1. In your slow cooker mix ghee with oil, turkey wings, cranberries, salt, pepper, onion, walnuts, orange juice and thyme, stir a bit, cover and cook on Low for 8 hours.
2. Divide turkey and orange sauce between plates and serve.
3. Enjoy!

Nutritional Value: Calories 300; Fat 12g; Carbohydrates 17g; Protein 1g

Recipe 89: Turkey Gumbo

Serving Size: 4

Cooking Time: 7 hours

Ingredients:

- 1 pound turkey wings
- Salt and black pepper to the taste
- 5 ounces water
- 1 yellow onion, chopped
- 1 yellow bell pepper, chopped
- 3 garlic cloves, chopped
- 2 tablespoons chili powder
- 1 and ½ teaspoons cumin, ground
- A pinch of cayenne pepper
- 2 cups veggies stock

Directions:

1. In your Slow cooker, mix turkey with salt, pepper, onion, bell pepper, garlic, chili powder, cumin, cayenne and stock, stir, cover and cook on Low for 7 hours.
2. Divide everything between plates and serve.

Nutritional Value: Calories 232; Fat 4g; Carbohydrates 17g; Protein 20g

Recipe 90: Winter Beef and Mushrooms

Serving Size: 4

Cooking Time: 7 hours

Ingredients:

- 3.5 ounces button mushrooms, sliced
- 3.5 ounces shiitake mushrooms, sliced
- 2 pounds beef shoulder, cut into medium cubes
- 16 ounces shallots, chopped
- 9 ounces beef stock
- 2 garlic cloves, minced
- 2 tablespoons chives, chopped
- 1 teaspoon sage, dried
- 1/8 teaspoon thyme, dried
- Salt and black pepper to the taste
- 3 and ½ tablespoons olive oil

Directions:

1. In your slow cooker, mix button mushrooms with shiitake mushrooms, beef, shallots, stock, garlic, chives, sage, thyme, salt, pepper and oil, toss, cover and cook on Low for 7 hours.
2. Divide beef and mushroom mix into plates and serve hot.
3. Enjoy!

Nutritional Value: Calories 362; Fat 7g; Carbohydrates 17g; Protein 37g

Chapter 5:   Dessert Recipes

Recipe 91: Apples with Raisins

Serving Size: 4

Cooking Time: 5 hours

Ingredients:

- 4 big apples
- 4 teaspoons raisins
- 4 teaspoons sugar
- ½ teaspoon ground cinnamon
- ½ cup of water

Directions:

1. Core the apples and fill them with sugar and raisins.
2. Then arrange the apples in the Slow Cooker.
3. Sprinkle them with ground cinnamon.
4. Add water and close the lid.
5. Cook the apples on low for 5 hours.

Nutritional Value: Calories 141; Fat 0.4g; Carbohydrates 37.4g; Protein 0.7g

Recipe 92: Banana Cookies

Serving Size: 4

Cooking Time: 2 hours

Ingredients:

- 2 bananas, mashed
- 1 egg, beaten
- 1 cup oatmeal
- 1 teaspoon ground cinnamon
- Cooking spray

Directions:

1. Mix bananas with egg and ground cinnamon.
2. Add oatmeal and whisk the mixture until smooth.
3. Then spray the Slow Cooker with cooking spray.
4. Make the cookies from the banana mixture with the help of the spoon and put them in the Slow Cooker.
5. Cook the cookies on High for 2 hours.

Nutritional Value: Calories 147; Fat 2.6g; Carbohydrates 27.9g; Protein 4.7g

Recipe 93: Maple Pears

Serving Size: 4

Cooking Time: 4 hours

Ingredients:

- 4 pears, peeled and tops cut off and cored
- 5 cardamom pods
- 2 cups orange juice
- ¼ cup maple syrup
- 1 cinnamon stick
- 1-inch ginger, grated

Directions:

1. Put the pears in your Slow cooker, add cardamom, orange juice, maple syrup, cinnamon and ginger, cover and cook on Low for 4 hours.
2. Divide pears between plates and serve them with the sauce on top.

Nutritional Value: Calories 200; Fat 4g; Carbohydrates 3g; Protein 4g

Recipe 94: Monkey Bread

Serving Size: 6

Cooking Time: 2 hours

Ingredients:

- 1 teaspoon cinnamon
- 1 cup brown sugar
- ¼ cup butter, melted
- 1 tube biscuits like Pillsbury Biscuits

Directions:

1. Break biscuits into the pre-cut pieces.
2. Mix the brown sugar and cinnamon.
3. Dip biscuit pieces into melted butter.
4. Put buttered biscuit into a bowl of cinnamon and brown sugar until fully coat.
5. Place the pieces into slow cooker until you have all of the pieces layered in the slow cooker.
6. Pour extra brown sugar and cinnamon on top.
7. Cook on LOW for 2 hours.
8. Serve.

Nutritional Value: Calories 368; Fat 9.2g; Carbohydrates 68.1g; Protein 5.1g

Recipe 95: Panna Cotta

Serving Size: 2

Cooking Time: 1 hour 30 minutes

Ingredients:

- 1 tablespoon gelatin
- 1 cup cream
- ¼ cup of sugar
- 2 tablespoons strawberry jam

Directions:

1. Pour cream in the Slow Cooker.
2. Add sugar and close the lid.
3. Cook the liquid on High for 1.5 hours.
4. Then cool it to the room temperature, add gelatin, and mix until smooth.
5. Pour the liquid in the glasses and refrigerate until solid.
6. Top every cream jelly with jam.

Nutritional Value: Calories 270; Fat 6.7g; Carbohydrates 47.4g; Protein 7g

Recipe 96: Peach Dump Cake

Serving Size: 6

Cooking Time: 4 hours

Ingredients:

- 4 cups frozen peaches
- 2 eggs
- 6 tablespoons butter, melted
- 1 (18.25 oz) box yellow cake mix
- ¼ teaspoon cinnamon
- ½ cup water

Directions:

1. Place frozen peaches in the bottom of the slow cooker.
2. Mix the cake mix with eggs, water and butter until smooth.
3. Spoon the batter over the peaches.
4. Sprinkle with cinnamon.
5. Cook for 4 hours on HIGH.
6. Serve warm.

Nutritional Value: Calories 211; Fat 23.4g; Carbohydrates 21g; Protein 6.8g

Recipe 97: Peach Pie

Serving Size: 4

Cooking Time: 4 hours

Ingredients:

- 4 cups peaches, peeled and sliced
- 1 cup sugar
- ½ teaspoon cinnamon powder
- 1 and ½ cups crackers, crushed
- ¼ teaspoon nutmeg, ground
- ½ cup milk
- 1 teaspoon vanilla extract
- Cooking spray

Directions:

2. In a bowl, mix peaches with half of the sugar and cinnamon and stir.
3. In another bowl, mix crackers with the rest of the sugar, nutmeg, milk and vanilla extract and stir.
4. Spray your Slow cooker with cooking spray, spread peaches on the bottom, add crackers mix, spread, cover and cook on Low for 4 hours.
5. Divide cobbler between plates and serve.

Nutritional Value: Calories 212; Fat 4g; Carbohydrates 7g; Protein 3g

Recipe 98: Peanut Butter Fudge Cake

Serving Size: 4

Cooking Time: 1 hour and 45 minutes

Ingredients:

- 1/3 cup of milk, 2%
- 1/4 cup of peanut butter, creamy
- 1 tablespoon of oil, canola
- 1/2 teaspoon of vanilla extract, pure
- 3/4 cup of sugar, granulated
- 1/2 cup of flour, all-purpose
- 3/4 teaspoon of baking powder
- 1 cup of water, boiling
- 2 tablespoon of cocoa, baking
- Optional: vanilla ice cream and chopped nuts for topping

Directions:

1. Grease a small-sized slow cooker with cooking spray.
2. In large-sized bowl, beat milk, oil, vanilla and peanut butter till blended well.
3. In smaller bowl, mix 1/4 cup of sugar with baking powder and flour and combine well. Beat this gradually into the milk mixture till blended well. Spread into small slow cooker.
4. In separate, small bowl, combine remainder of sugar with the cocoa. Add boiling water and stir. Pour in slow cooker without stirring once it's in there.
5. Cover slow cooker. Cook on the high setting for 1 to 1 & 1/2 hours, till you can insert a toothpick in middle and have it come back clean. Serve while warm.

Nutritional Value: Calories 217; Fat 16.3g; Carbohydrates 3.4g; Protein 14.7g

Recipe 99: Pudding Cake

Serving Size: 8

Cooking Time: 2 hours 30 minutes

Ingredients:

- 1 and ½ cup sugar
- 1 cup flour
- ¼ cup cocoa powder+ 2 tablespoons
- ½ cup chocolate almond milk
- 2 teaspoons baking powder
- 2 tablespoons vegetable oil
- 1 teaspoon vanilla extract
- 1 and ½ cups hot water
- Cooking spray

Directions:

1. In a bowl, mix flour with 2 tablespoons cocoa, baking powder, milk, oil and vanilla extract, whisk well and spread on the bottom of the Slow cooker, greased with cooking spray.
2. In another bowl, mix sugar with the rest of the cocoa and the water, whisk well, spread over the batter in the Slow cooker, cover, cook your cake on High for 2 hours and 30 minutes.
3. Leave the cake to actually cool down, slice and serve.

Nutritional Value: Calories 250; Fat 4g; Carbohydrates 40g; Protein 4g

Recipe 100:   Stuffed Apples

Serving Size: 5

Cooking Time: 1 hour 30 minutes

Ingredients:

- 5 apples, tops cut off and cored
- 5 figs
- 1/3 cup sugar
- 1 teaspoon dried ginger
- ¼ cup pecans, chopped
- 2 teaspoons lemon zest, grated
- ¼ teaspoon nutmeg, ground
- ½ teaspoon cinnamon powder
- 1 tablespoon lemon juice
- 1tablespoon vegetable oil
- ½ cup water

Directions:

1. In a bowl, mix figs with sugar, ginger, pecans, lemon zest, nutmeg, cinnamon, oil and lemon juice, whisk really well, stuff your apples with this mix and put them in your Slow cooker.
2. Add the water, cover, cook on High for 1 hour and 30 minutes, divide between dessert plates and serve.

Nutritional Value: Calories 200; Fat 1g; Carbohydrates 4g; Protein 7g

6.   Conclusion

Collecting 100 slow cooker recipes between its pages this slow cooker cookbook shows what it's like to be an invaluable home cook's handbook for every possible cooking occasion. Chop up your ingredients, mix them well, load your slow cooker and allow it to do the hardest part! Family-friendly recipes are a perfect choice to make as they require fairly basic cooking skills, are low on cleanup and help you to eat a little bit healthier every day!

It's a weeknight game changer with all the nutritional info and all the necessary cooking directions you can think about. Let your perfect dinner simmer on its own while you are running your errands, spending hours with your family or simply enjoying your time. You should know that these recipes come together perfectly not only in a slow cooker but on a stovetop as well. Subtly balanced taste and nutritional value will make it easy for you to enjoy your meals with all the right to do so.

Initiate a positive, well-organized approach towards the cooking style you've only just discovered. It's a revolution of slow cooking in every possible way. You must set aside all the templates you've been using before and dive into our most-requested recipes that will surely become mainstays in your household too. Thoughtfully selected breakfasts, main and side dishes, snacks, desserts; you'll find plenty of options to choose from! This is the taste and the quality your family will vote for.

7. Index

Made in the USA
Las Vegas, NV
01 December 2022

60542657R00063